INSIDE THE SEATTLE STORM

ANNE E. HILL

Lerner Publications ◆ Minneapolis

Lerner Publications Company
An imprint of Lerner Publishing Group, Inc.
241 First Avenue North
Minneapolis, MN 55401 USA

For reading levels and more information, look up this title at www.lernerbooks.com.

Main body text set in Aptifer Slab LT Pro / Typeface provided by Linotype AG

Library of Congress Cataloging-in-Publication Data

Names: Hill, Anne E., 1974– author.
Title: Inside the Seattle Storm / Anne E. Hill.
Description: Minneapolis : Lerner Publications, 2023. | Series: Super sports teams | Includes bibliographical references and index. | Audience: Ages 7–11 | Audience: Grades 4–6 | Summary: "The Seattle Storm have never lost a WNBA championship series. Follow the Storm from their first season to becoming four-time WNBA champions, and read about nail-biting games, surprising victories, and the team's biggest stars"— Provided by publisher.
Identifiers: LCCN 2022011909 (print) | LCCN 2022011910 (ebook) | ISBN 9781728476117 (library binding) | ISBN 9781728478692 (paperback) | ISBN 9781728485263 (ebook)
Subjects: LCSH: Seattle Storm (Basketball team)—Juvenile literature. | Women's National Basketball Association—Juvenile literature.
Classification: LCC GV885.52.S295 H55 2023 (print) | LCC GV885.52.S295 (ebook) | DDC 796.323/6409797772—dc23/eng/20220604

LC record available at https://lccn.loc.gov/2022011909
LC ebook record available at https://lccn.loc.gov/2022011910

TABLE OF CONTENTS

FOUR-TIME FINALISTS 4
A STORMY HISTORY 9
AMAZING MOMENTS 15
STORM SUPERSTARS 19
THE ROAD AHEAD 25

Storm Season Record Holders 28
Glossary 30
Learn More 31
Index 32

Breanna Stewart (*right*) averaged 19.7 points per game for the Seattle Storm during the 2020 season.

FOUR-TIME FINALISTS

FACTS AT A GLANCE

- The **STORM** won the Women's National Basketball Association (WNBA) Championship in 2004, 2010, 2018, and 2020.
- The team plays at **CLIMATE PLEDGE ARENA** in Seattle, Washington.
- The Storm is one of two teams that have never lost in the **WNBA FINALS**.
- **LAUREN JACKSON'S** number 15 jersey is the team's only retired number.

The Seattle Storm had already been champions. They had reached the WNBA Finals three times. They won all three series, but the 2020 Finals were not like other years. The COVID-19 pandemic had forced all of the league's teams to protect the players and coaches. They had moved to the IMG Academy in Bradenton, Florida. They stayed away from other people to keep everyone healthy and safe.

The Storm were playing far from home, but they were still a tough team to beat in the playoffs. They entered the Finals against the top-seeded Las Vegas Aces. The Storm were the underdogs, but they still beat the Aces. Two big reasons for their win were star players Breanna Stewart and Sue Bird. Stewart led the team in points, and Bird led in assists. In their third and final game to win the championship, the Storm forced 18 turnovers.

When the game clock stopped at the end of Game 3, the Storm had made history. They beat the Aces 92–59. The Storm won by 33 points! That was the biggest victory in WNBA Finals history. But the Storm had not always been such a strong team. They had come a long way since their start as the Seattle Reign.

Sue Bird (*right*) is the first WNBA player to win a championship in three different decades.

The Storm defeated the Aces in just three games in the 2020 WNBA Finals.

Kate Paye takes the ball down the court during the Storm's first season as a team.

A STORMY HISTORY

The Seattle Storm franchise began in 1996 as the Seattle Reign in the American Basketball League. That league ended in 1998 and the Storm moved to the WNBA. In 2000, they had their first season in their new league. The Storm had a disappointing 6–26 record that year. However, that gave them the first overall pick of the 2001 WNBA Draft. They chose 19-year-old Lauren Jackson, a young and impressive player from Australia. With Jackson, the team had a better 10–22 record in the 2001 season.

Lauren Jackson spent her entire 13-season career with the Seattle Storm.

In 2002, University of Connecticut (UCONN) star Sue Bird joined the Storm. That year, the team made the playoffs for the first time. Just two years later, the Storm won their first WNBA Championship. Anne Donovan, the Storm's coach, became the first woman head coach in league history to win a championship.

The Storm picked Bird first overall in the 2002 WNBA Draft.

Breanna Stewart (*right*) was named one of the WNBA's top 25 players of the league's first 25 years in 2021.

The Storm had some ups and downs until 2010, when they won their second championship. After that, the team changed coaches, and many of the team's players were injured. Following a disappointing record in 2015, they drafted Breanna Stewart, another UCONN star. The Storm worked hard to improve and won championships in 2018 and 2020. This made the Storm the most successful pro sports team ever to play in Seattle.

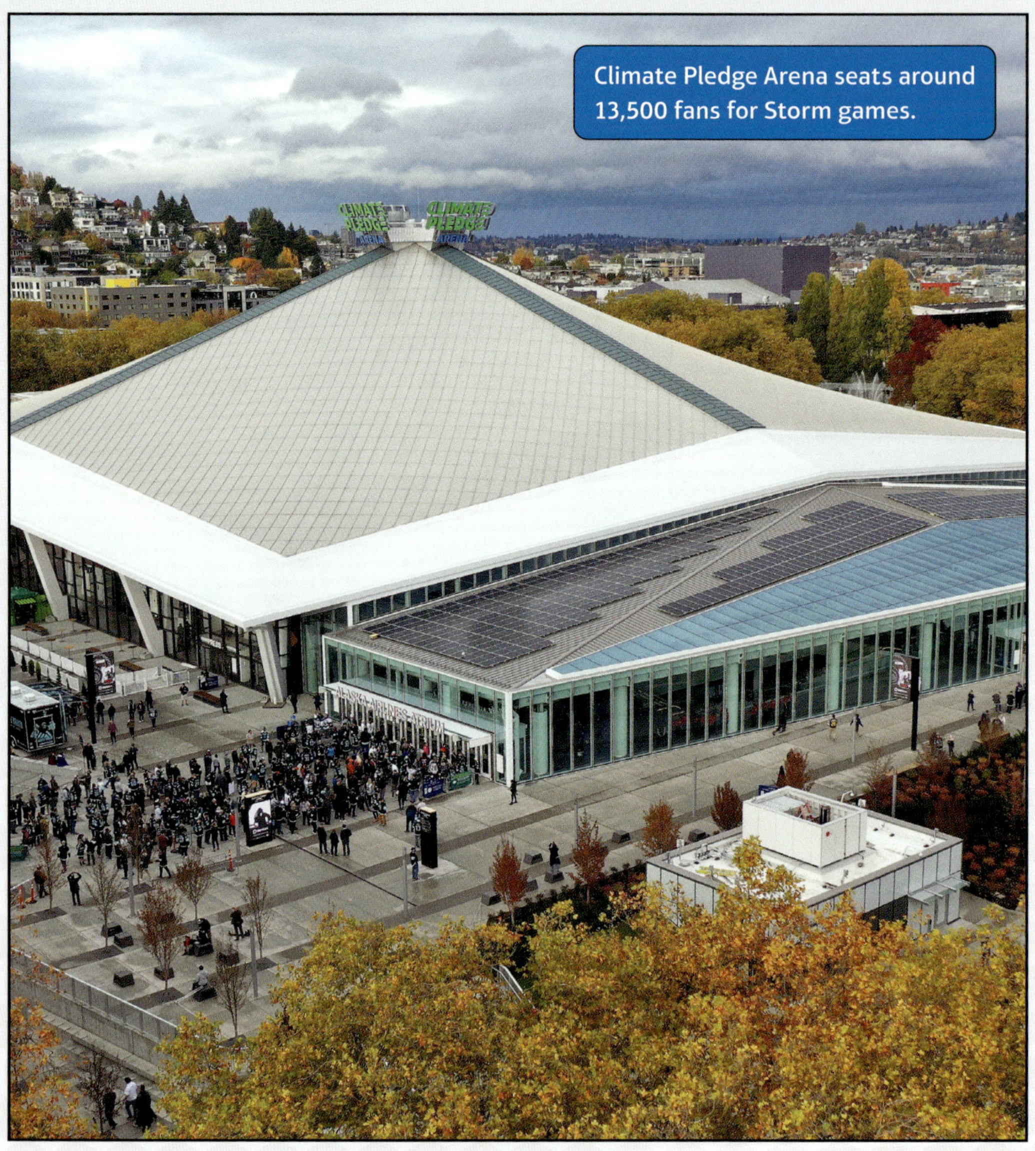

Climate Pledge Arena seats around 13,500 fans for Storm games.

The Storm almost left Seattle in 2006 when the team was sold to a company in Oklahoma City, Oklahoma. Force 10 Hoops, a group of women business owners in Seattle, bought the team and kept them in the city. The team plays home games at Climate Pledge Arena, the first pro sports arena in the world powered by only solar and wind energy.

STORM FACT

The Storm got their name from the rainy weather of Seattle. Their mascot Doppler is named after a type of radar used to track storms.

Doppler helps pump up the team's fans during games.

Jackson (*center, holding trophy*) ranked first in the WNBA for points scored during the 2004 season.

AMAZING MOMENTS

With 16 trips to the WNBA playoffs and four championships since 2000, the Storm have given Seattle a lot to cheer about. The Storm's 2004 season started slow, but it ended with a thrilling finish to advance to the Finals. They faced the Connecticut Sun in three close games.

The Sun took the first game 68–64. Then the Storm beat the Sun 67–65 in Game 2. In Game 3, the Sun focused on defending Storm stars Sue Bird and Lauren Jackson. This allowed the Storm's new team member, Betty Lennox, to put up 23 points. Lennox helped lead the Storm to a 74–60 championship win.

Betty Lennox (*left*) was named MVP of the 2004 WNBA Finals.

In 2010, the team was on fire from the start. They had a 28–6 season record and a perfect home record of 17–0. That is the most home wins in the history of the WNBA. Even though the Storm won the conference finals, the championship series against the Atlanta Dream was tough. All three games came down to close finishes in the final seconds of play. But each time, the Storm were the winners. The Storm were champions again, and they were the first WNBA team to go 7–0 in the playoffs.

Jewell Loyd was the number one overall pick in the 2015 WNBA Draft.

In 2018, the Storm played against the Washington Mystics in the Finals. The Storm had played hard in the playoffs. Standout player Bird broke her nose during one game. But she still managed to help the team against the Phoenix Mercury. Seattle's 89–76 win in Game 1 included 23 points from Jewell Loyd and 22 points from Stewart. Game 2 was a nail-biting 75–73 win by the Storm. The Storm took Game 3 with a solid 98–82 win. Stewart had an impressive 30 points while teammate Natasha Howard had 29. The Storm were champions again!

The 2020 season was shorter than usual because of the COVID-19 pandemic. But the Storm played well and made it to the Finals. There, they faced the Aces.

When the Storm had played the Aces earlier in the season, they had lost. Bird and Stewart had not played due to injuries. Their addition in the Finals made all the difference for Seattle. The Storm easily defeated the Aces in three games. In 2021, the Storm visited the White House and became the first women's sports team to be honored by President Joe Biden.

STORM FACT

At home games, the Storm has a dance squad made up of kids. They bring young fans onto the court to dance during breaks in the action.

The Storm presented President Joe Biden with a number 46 jersey during their White House visit in 2021.

Bird is the WNBA's all-time leader in assists and has been named to 12 All-Star teams.

STORM SUPERSTARS

The Seattle Storm owes its success to an incredible group of owners, coaches, and players. The Storm is owned by four Seattle businesspeople: Lisa Brummel, Ginny Gilder, Anne Levinson, and Dawn Trudeau.

Lin Dunn (*left*) brought 30 years of coaching experience to the Storm when she became head coach in 2000.

Lin Dunn coached the Storm from 2000 to 2003. She was the team's first head coach. After her, Anne Donovan became coach and helped the team win its first championship. Donovan stayed with the Storm from 2003 to 2007. The team's current head coach is former Storm player Noelle Quinn.

The Storm's first star player was Lauren Jackson, who started with the team in 2001. She retired from the WNBA in 2012. Her number (15) is the team's only retired jersey number. To honor Jackson, no Storm player will ever wear 15 during a game again. Jackson led the Storm in points and assists per game for 10 seasons. She was an All-Star eight times and won the WNBA Most Valuable Player award three times.

At 6 feet, 6 inches (2 m) tall, Jackson was a force to be reckoned with on the court.

STORM FACT

The logo and colors of the Storm have changed over the years. Their current logo is yellow and green and features Seattle's famous Space Needle tower.

Former Storm point guard Noelle Quinn became the team's head coach in 2021.

Sue Bird and Jackson became an unstoppable pair once Bird joined the team in 2002. For 17 of her 20 seasons with the Storm, Bird has led the team in assists per game. At 41, she is also the oldest player in the league. After more than 20 years playing pro women's basketball, Bird is not slowing down.

Natasha Howard had one of the best seasons of her pro career with the Storm in 2019.

Breanna Stewart burst onto the scene in 2016 and has been a star player ever since. In five of her six seasons with the Storm, she has led in points and rebounds per game. She won the 2016 Rookie of the Year award and is a three-time All-Star. Like her teammates Bird and Jackson, Stewart has also played in the Olympic Games for Team USA.

While the Storm's most well-known names may be Jackson, Bird, and Stewart, the team has had other great players over the years. These include Kamila Vodičková, Natasha Howard, Tanisha Wright, and Swin Cash. Jordin Canada and Jewell Loyd are current standouts.

Jordin Canada averaged 2.3 steals per game for the Storm in the 2019 season.

Bird is considered one of the best point guards in the history of pro basketball.

THE ROAD AHEAD

In the season after their 2020 WNBA Championship, the Storm were one of the league's top teams. Sadly, Stewart was injured and missed the final games of the season and the playoffs. The Storm's season was cut short in the second round of the playoffs.

Even though they ended the 2021 season with a loss, the future looks bright for the Storm. They have star players Stewart and Lloyd, who have already helped their team win two WNBA titles. They also have basketball legend Sue Bird leading the team. Fans call these three players Seattle's "Big Three."

With an all-star lineup and exciting new players, the Storm hopes to win a fifth WNBA Championship.

Almost every year, the Storm is a winning team. The Seattle Storm is the only existing WNBA team that has never lost a championship. The Storm inspires young basketball fans in Seattle and around the world.

Mercedes Russell helped the Storm win a championship in her first year as a pro.

Ezi Magbegor played pro basketball in Australia before joining the Storm in 2020.

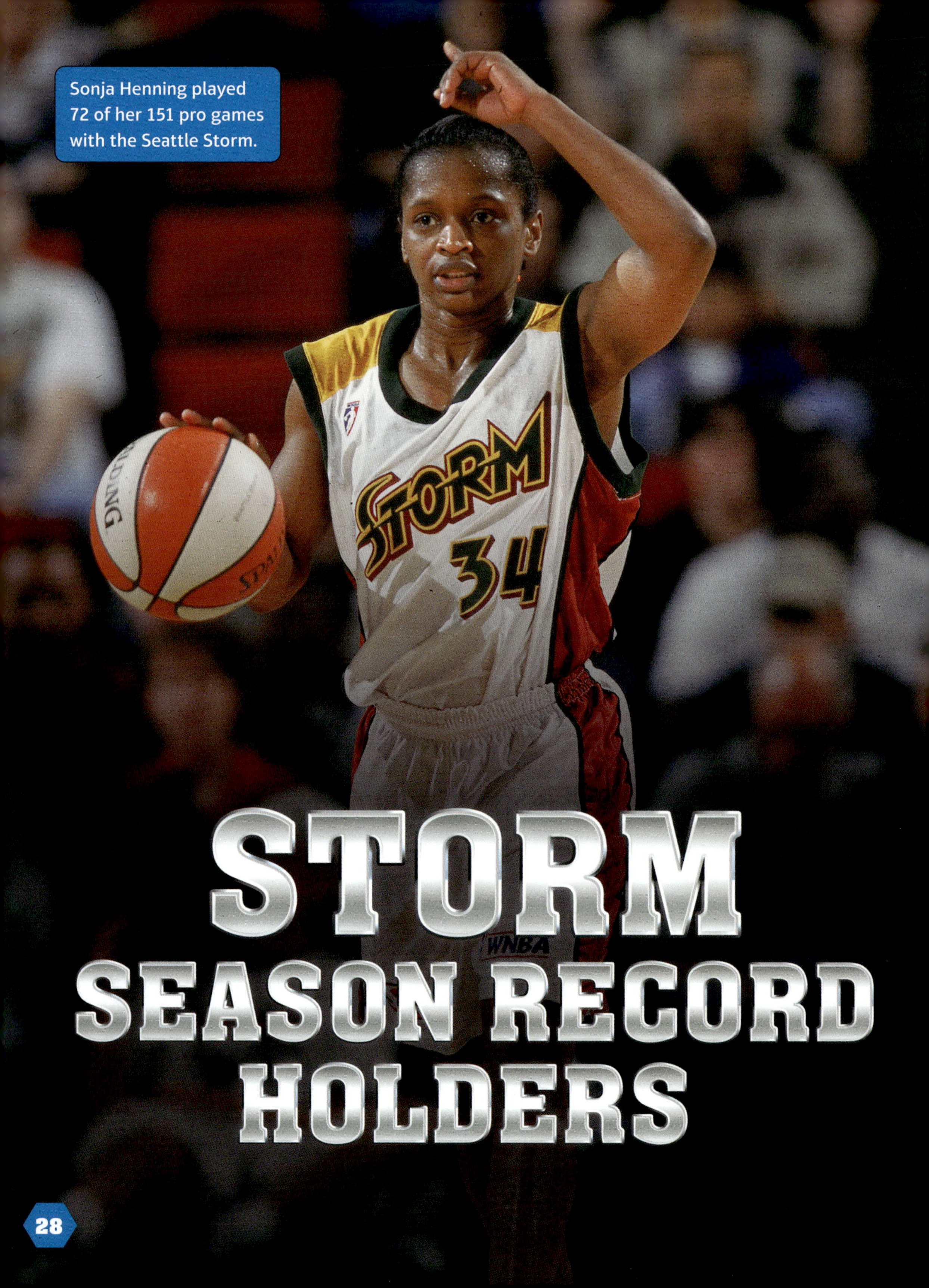

Sonja Henning played 72 of her 151 pro games with the Seattle Storm.

STORM SEASON RECORD HOLDERS

POINTS

1. Breanna Stewart, 742 (2018)
2. Lauren Jackson, 739 (2007)
3. Lauren Jackson, 698 (2003)
4. Lauren Jackson, 656 (2010)
   Breanna Stewart, 656 (2017)
5. Lauren Jackson, 634 (2004)

ASSISTS

1. Sue Bird, 221 (2003)
   Sue Bird, 221 (2018)
2. Sue Bird, 199 (2017)
3. Sue Bird, 196 (2016)
4. Sue Bird, 191 (2002)
5. Sue Bird, 190 (2010)

REBOUNDS

1. Breanna Stewart, 317 (2016)
2. Lauren Jackson, 313 (2005)
3. Lauren Jackson, 307 (2003)
4. Lauren Jackson, 300 (2007)
5. Breanna Stewart, 287 (2017)

BLOCKED SHOTS

1. Lauren Jackson, 81 (2002)
2. Lauren Jackson, 67 (2005)
   Natasha Howard, 67 (2018)
3. Lauren Jackson, 64 (2001)
   Lauren Jackson, 64 (2003)
   Breanna Stewart, 64 (2016)

STEALS

1. Natasha Howard, 74 (2019)
2. Jordin Canada, 68 (2019)
3. Sonja Henning, 61 (2000)
   Sue Bird, 61 (2006)
4. Sue Bird, 55 (2002)
   Camille Little, 55 (2010)

THREE-POINT BASKETS

1. Sue Bird, 72 (2016)
2. Sue Bird, 71 (2011)
3. Jewell Loyd, 67 (2018)
   Sue Bird, 67 (2021)
4. Jewell Loyd, 65 (2021)

GLOSSARY

assist: a pass from a teammate that leads directly to a score

draft: when teams take turns choosing new players

Finals: the WNBA's Championship series

franchise: a sports team and the people who own and operate it

mascot: a person, animal, or object used as a symbol to represent a sports team and to bring good luck

pandemic: an outbreak of a disease over a wide area that affects many people

top-seed: the player or team with the best record

underdog: a team or player thought to have little chance of winning

turnover: losing possession of the ball to the opposing team

LEARN MORE

ESPN—WNBA
https://www.espn.com/wnba/

Fishman, Jon M. *Breanna Stewart*. Minneapolis: Lerner Publications, 2019.

Hill, Christina. *Sue Bird*. Minneapolis: Lerner Publications, 2022.

Schaller, Bob. *The Everything Kids' Basketball Book: The All-Time Greats, Legendary Teams, Today's Superstars—and Tips on Playing Like a Pro*. New York: Adams Media, 2019.

Seattle Storm—Team Stats
https://storm.wnba.com/stats/

Sports Illustrated Kids—Basketball
https://www.sikids.com/basketball

INDEX

American Basketball League, 9

Bird, Sue, 5, 10, 15–17, 21, 23, 25, 29

Climate Pledge Arena, 5, 12

Donovan, Anne, 10, 20

Doppler, 11

Force 10 Hoops, 12

Jackson, Lauren, 5, 9, 15, 20–21, 23, 29

Quinn, Noelle, 20–21

Stewart, Breanna, 5, 11, 16–17, 23, 25, 29

Women's National Basketball Association (WNBA), 5–6, 9–11, 15–16, 20, 25–26

PHOTO ACKNOWLEDGMENTS

Image credits: Julio Aguilar/Stringer/Getty Images, p.4; Julio Aguilar/Stringer/Getty Images, p.6; Julio Aguilar/Stringer/Getty Images, p.7; Todd Warshaw/Staff/Getty Images, p.8; Chuck Myers/MCT/Newscom, p.9; Lisa Blumenfeld/Staff/Getty Images, p.10; Mike Carlson/Stringer/Getty Images, p.11; Bruce Bennett/Staff/Getty Images, p.12; Andrew Fredrickson/ZUMApress/Newscom, p.13; Otto Greule Jr/Stringer/Getty Images, p.14; Chris Trotman/Stringer/Getty Images, p.15; Ethan Miller/Staff/Getty Images, p.16; Drew Angerer/Staff/Getty Images, p.17; Steph Chambers/Staff/Getty Images, p.18; Otto Greule Jr/Stringer/Getty Images, p.19; Otto Greule Jr/Stringer/Getty Images, p.20; Steph Chambers/Staff/Getty Images, p.21; Abbie Parr/Stringer/Getty Images, p.22; Katharine Lotze/Staff/Getty Images, p.23; Steph Chambers/Staff/Getty Images, 24; Steph Chambers/Staff/Getty Images, p.25; Steph Chambers/Staff/Getty Images, p.26; Steph Chambers/Staff/Getty Images, p.27; Otto Greule Jr/Stringer/Getty Images, p.28

Design element: Master3D/Shutterstock.com.

Cover image: Christian Petersen/Staff/Getty Images